WINDS
of
FAVOR

Michelle J. Miller

WINDS OF FAVOR by Michelle J. Miller
Second Edition
Published by Michelle J. Miller
www.michellejmiller.global

Unless otherwise noted, all Scripture quotations are taken from the King James Version of the Bible.

Scripture quotations marked by AMP are from the Amplified Bible. Copyright © 2015 by The Lockton Foundation. Used by permission. All rights reserved.

Scripture quotations marked NJKV are taken from the New King James Version of the Bible. Copyright © 1982 by Thomas Nelson. Used by permission. All rights reserved.

Visit the author's website at www.michellejmiller.global

Printed in the United States of America

WINDS OF FAVOR

Dedication

I dedicate this book to my spiritual father, Apostle John Eckhardt. Apostle Eckhardt, thank you for encouraging people around the world to believe God for "Ridiculous Favor".

Table of Contents

INTRODUCTION

Winds are powerful. The Hebrew word for wind is "Ruach". Ruach, Strong's 7307, means breath, wind, spirit. When we read about ruach in the bible we are reading about the powerful activity of God. God causes the wind (ruach) to blow over the earth (Genesis 8:1). In Genesis 8:1, God caused a wind to blow on the earth to stop the flood. Weather events are examples of God's activity on the earth. If you consider the impact of many weather events, it is the wind that has the greatest impact. I have a special personal, professional and spiritual understanding of winds and favor. I have always asked and prayed for favor. There were times in my life when I had few connections and very little money, but I knew to pray for the light of God's favor to shine upon my life (Job 22:28 AMP). I have always prayed for favor, but my understanding of favor greatly increased while my pastor was doing a thirty (30) day teaching about favor on Facebook and Periscope. My revelatory understanding of winds helped me to grasp the importance and impact of a prophetic word God gave me entitled "Winds of Favor" in July 2017. The strength of the prophecy was so significant that it became the title of this book.

I personally understand the power of wind. I was born and raised in Chicago, Illinois. Chicago is known as the "Windy City." If you ever visit Chicago, especially in the winter, you will understand why Chicago is known as the Windy City. Chicago can be very cold in the winter, but what makes the winter almost unbearable to some people is the wind. When the winds blow in Chicago they get your attention. The winds of Chicago will push you forward. The winds of Chicago make mild weather events extreme. The winds of Chicago have a lot of strength and power. If you're walking along the streets of Chicago and the winds blow it is a mind boggling experience. God is releasing winds of favor akin to the winds of Chicago. Just as Chicago winds are strong and powerful so are the winds of favor. The winds of favor will push you forward, cause you to step out in extreme faith and give your life a mind boggling change.

Professionally, I also understand the impact of winds. I'm a corporate attorney by profession and one of my responsibilities is being the primary counsel for over 26 states in the U.S.A, Puerto Rico, Guam, the U.S. Virgin Islands and the America Samoa. One of my busiest times is when severe weather events occur in one of these jurisdictions. Severe weather events such as hurricanes, tornadoes, typhoons are all wind related weather events that often times change the course of people's lives and businesses. I have to give expedient legal advice and make strategic decisions to help guide my business leaders when a severe weather event occurs. There's no time to be indecisive or double-minded because the strong winds are causing rapid change. Are you having a hard time making decisions and stepping out in faith? The winds of favor are about to blow strongly in your life and there's no time to procrastinate. You must stop waiting for confirmation after confirmation after confirmation. You may not need another confirmation, you need the courage to make a decision to believe God and step out in faith. There's no time to be double-minded, you must move with the wind. You can try to stand still when the winds of favor our blowing, but just like the powerful winds in Chicago move people, the winds of favor will move you.

Spiritually, winds are important. The word "favor" is found almost 300 times in the Amplified Bible so you can meditate on a scripture on favor almost every day of the year! The word "wind" appears in the King James Version of the Bible 113 times and the word "winds" appear 22 times. The Hebrew word "Ruach" (Strong's #7307) means breath, wind, spirit. When the wind of God is blowing it can also be reflective of the breath of God or the spirit of God. Winds also represent the power and presence of God on the earth.

Can you imagine God blowing His breath from the heavens on you and releasing favor upon you? I hope you can. God spoke the world into existence, He didn't have to do anything but open His mouth. In Acts 2, the Holy Spirit came like a mighty rushing wind. In Acts 2 the wind of God appeared as the power of God. Favor is coming upon your life like a mighty rushing wind. The power of God is going to be demonstrated in your life because His favor upon you will suddenly transform your life. God's power and presence is about to be revealed in your life as the winds of favor blow your way.

Wind has power and significance. In this book you'll read about the different winds of favor that God is blowing over His people. This book is mostly a collection of prophecies that God gave me on favor. However, I also expound on various scriptures and aspects of favor. This is your set time of favor.

Embrace your season of favor and walk in it without apology. Winds of flavor are blowing your way. Do not seek shelter from the winds, stand in the winds and let God wrap His favor all around you. In this book you will read the different kinds of favor that He is releasing into the lives of His faithful servants. Embrace the winds of favor described in this book.

1

LIGHT OF GOD'S FAVOR

*You shall also decide and decree a thing, and it shall be
established for you; and the light [of God's favor] shall shine upon
your ways.*
- Job 22:28 (AMP)

The light of God's favor is shining brightly . The
light of God's favor is glorious. The light of God's
favor is amazing. When the light of God's favor is upon
your life and it shines upon your ways, you will never be
the same. The light of God's favor causes you to stand
out in the crowd, when you walk into a room people
recognize that you are not like everyone else. The light
of God's favor was upon the life of Esther, although
she was one of many women she was seen as a one of a
kind woman to the king. Esther had favor with the king

and her life is an example of the kind of favor we have with the King of kings.

There were times in my life when I knew things happened in my life because the light of God's favor was shining upon my life. Others that witnessed the light of God's favor on my life thought that I had secret connections or close relationships with people that I barely knew. I always gave glory to God and attributed unexpected blessings to my meditation and prayers in alignment with Job 22:28. There will be times in you life when great things will occur and the only feasible explanation for them occurring is the blessings and favor of God.

The light of God's favor had to be upon Esther in order for her to experience the favor of the king. Because the king loved Esther above all women she found favor in his sight (Esther 2:17). In fact, everyone that saw Esther favored her (Esther 2:15). When the light of God's favor is upon your ways, nothing can stand in your way. People will grant your requests and extend special privileges to you when the light of God's favor is upon your life. Some of us are too afraid to ask for things. Esther was afraid to go before the king and humbly present herself at his throne. Well, after a time of fasting and prayer, Esther boldly went into to the king's presence and approached his throne to request favor.

> So it was, when the king saw Queen Esther standing in the court, that she found favor in his sight, and the king held out to Esther the golden scepter that was in his hand. Then Esther went near and touched the top of the

scepter. – Esther 5:2(NKJV)

The king granted Esther's request because she was favored. Do not be afraid to approach God's throne of favor because it is His pleasure to bestow His favor upon you. The favor of God was not just for Esther, it had a greater purpose and that purpose was to save her people. When God bestows favor upon your life, it is not just for you, it is for you to release favor upon others as well. Never be stingy when God's favor is upon your life. The favor of God upon your life can change the lives of others, just as the favor of God upon Esther's life saved her and her people.

> Then Queen Esther answered and said, "If I have found favor in your sight, O king, and if it pleases the king, let my life be given me at my petition, and my people at my request.
> – Esther 7:3 (NKJV)

Approach the King's throne. Boldly go before God's throne of favor, don't be afraid. Join a growing number of people who are diligently asking God to shine the light of His favor upon them just as many asked in the Book of Psalms:

> Many are asking, "Who will help us to see better days?" LORD, may the light of your favor shine upon us. – Psalms 4:6 (NKJV)

As you enter into the presence of God, as you go before His throne, He will shine His light upon you. After you humbly go before God's throne of favor, you will leave the presence of God with the light of His favor shining upon your life.

Prophetic Exhortation & Prophecy:

God is shining His light of favor upon His people in the middle of the year. The light of God's favor will highlight you, it will cause you to stand out.

You may have been praying for better days. When the light of God's favor shines on you, your days will change. Days of sorrow will become days of joy. Days of frustration will become days of peace. The light of God's favor transforms how you see yourself and how others see you. The light of God's favor will open doors for you that no man can shut. The light of God's favor will promote you and bring you before great men and women.

The light of God's favor is divine favor; this favor brings benefits. The light of God's favor brings blessings. The light of God's favor will cause you to have favor in the sight of people in your midst. You will change the very atmosphere of places you go because the light of God's favor is shining upon you. While others are lost in the darkness of life the light of God's favor will illuminate a pathway for you. When people try to bring you down the light of God's favor will lift you up.

These are the days of the light of God's favor. You will intercede for people and because of the light of God's favor upon your life, your prayers will be answered. Those who need healing (physical, mental, emotional) will come to you and ask you to seek the light of God's favor on their behalf and when you do God will restore them. The light of God's favor is not just for you; the light of God's favor demonstrates to the world the majesty of God.

God is showing up to release the light of His favor. Do not miss your set time of favor due to doubt and the unbelief. The light of God's favor is being released now so position yourself to receive it.

- FAVOR MEDITATION -

You shall also decide and decree a thing, and it shall be established for you; and the light [of God's favor] shall shine upon your ways. When they make [you] low, you will say, [There is] a lifting up; and the humble person He lifts up and saves. He will even deliver the one [for whom you intercede] who is not innocent; yes, he will be delivered through the cleanness of your hands.
- Job 22:28-30 (AMP)

WINDS OF FAVOR

2

ABSOLUTE FAVOR

*And the angel said to her, Do not be afraid, Mary, for you have
found grace (free, spontaneous, absolute favor and loving-kindness)
with God.*
- Luke 1:30 (AMP)

Absolute favor is unrestrained favor. When the
winds of absolute favor blow in your life no one can
limit the level of favor that God puts on your life. God
wants you to experience favor that is not limited in any
way. There is a wind of absolute favor blowing. There is
a wind of outright favor blowing. God told me that this
wind of favor is akin to outright property ownership.
When you have outright ownership of a property you
have absolute ownership. In order to understand the
wind of "absolute favor" it is important to understand
the meaning of the word "absolute" which is defined
below:

free from imperfection; complete; not mixed or adulterated; pure; outright; free from restriction and limitation; not limited in any way, unrestrained; viewed independently; not comparative or relative; ultimate (dictionary. com)

God is releasing favor without restriction or limitation. Winds of favor are blowing freely simply because we serve a good God. Absolute ownership of a property means there are no constraints to your ownership, you do not need to do anything to secure your property ownership status, you have it. Outright, absolute ownership does not require any additional payments, the price has been paid. One way that you can own property outright is to inherit it. No one can take property from you when you own the property outright because your ownership is absolute. So it is with absolute favor. We all have a level of absolute favor that we inherited through Jesus Christ.

Jesus is the heir of all things (Hebrews 1:2). The Father has given Him all things (John 3:35). We are part of a royal priesthood and Jesus is the great high priest (Hebrews 4:14). We are heirs of the Kingdom and as heirs there are some things God will give to us just because we are His sons and daughters. There is no restraint on the winds of favor that are blowing right now. The absolute favor that God has for you is for you; no one can take away your favor.

Absolute favor belongs to you outright. Jesus already paid the price for you to receive absolute favor. You are an inheritor of the Kingdom and absolute favor is included in your inheritance. Jesus came that you may have an abundant life. A life of absolute favor is an abundant life. You may feel as if you don't deserve to have this wind of favor blow over your life, but you do. There are things you can do to receive favor, but God also want you to know there are times when He will just give you favor because He is a good God.

Prophetic Exhortation & Prophecy:

When I was commanding my morning in prayer, I heard the word "absolute" so I pulled up the definition and when I read it I just shouted hallelujah, When God releases favor on His chosen vessels it is absolute!

In the middle year God is releasing pure favor, favor that is perfect for your life's purpose. There's no limitation to and no restriction on absolute favor - God releases it freely so that you can run the race set before you in faith. The absolute favor released upon your life is independent of what God released on the lives of others. This is not a favor competition, says God. The favor I have for you is for you! No one can stop its release and no one can take it. Absolute favor is ultimate favor - it catapults you into your destiny thereby becoming the catalyst for the manifestation of your visions and dreams. Absolute favor launches you into a lifestyle of continuous favor. When I received this prophetic word about absolute favor, I thought of that bunny on that old Duracell commercial - your favor is going to go on and on and on and on!

Absolute favor has no strings attached, you have already positioned yourself to receive it as a humble servant. You must die to self to receive this level of favor and once you do I can trust you with it says God. I see your heart, says the Lord. Because your heart is towards Me and My Kingdom purposes, absolute favor is your portion. Yes, some of you have been selected for absolute favor.

God says my absolute favor is genuine. It positions

you to do exactly what I purposed for you to do. Absolute favor is sure favor - without a doubt you know that it comes from Me, says God. You will say WOW, THIS IS SURELY THE FAVOR OF GOD! You have no other explanation for the absolute favor you will experience. You will proclaim his is the Lord's doing and many will acknowledge Me because of what they see Me do for and through you says the Lord.

People may want to restrict this favor, but they can't. People may think you are not qualified for this favor, but so what! God said you met the qualifications of this favor in the secret place. God says you were just being you - a humble, trustworthy, giving and prayerful servant. My absolute favor is the unexpected outcome of your faithfulness. This favor brings forth strong deliverance in masses. This favor confines the minds of men.

Many women (and men) have done noble things, but you SURPASS them all. Yes, many have done well, but you excel them all. Many have been called, but you were chosen amongst them all.

I'm about to go all out for you says God because you go all out for me. My absolute favor is no joke! There no holds barred! There's no ifs or buts about it! This favor liberates you and I release my absolute favor freely to my chosen ones says the Lord.

- FAVOR MEDITATION -

And blessed [spiritually fortunate and favored by God] is she who believed and confidently trusted that there would be a fulfillment of the things that were spoken to her [by the angel sent] from the Lord."
— Luke 1:45 (AMP)

WINDS OF FAVOR

3

UNLIMITED FAVOR

I pray that from his glorious, unlimited resources he will empower
you with inner strength through his Spirit.
- Ephesians 3:16(NLT)

Take the limits off! The winds of unlimited favor
are causing the removal of limitations on your life. God
is El Shaddai, the God that is more than enough and He
gives favor to us freely from His unlimited resources.
God has more than enough favor to distribute as He
pleases on the earth. God's resources are unlimited and
His favor is unlimited. God does not run out of favor.
At times you may feel like you do not have favor the
favor of God on your life, but do not let these feelings
distract you from the reality that God has more than
enough favor for you and everyone else on the earth.
You must believe that the Lord is your shepherd and
you shall not want (Ps. 23:1). There will never be a favor

shortage. You will never get to a point in your life where there is a favor drought. God's favor does not run out.

God wants us to experience a continuous flow of favor. There is a secret to experiencing unlimited favor and that secret is to consistently release favor. God will provide favor in a multitude of ways so pray for God to release His unlimited favor in your life by any means necessary. God wants you to be a giver of favor. As God gives you favor He wants you to give favor. God will release favor into the lives of others for your sake. God blessed Laban for Joseph's sake. Laban's association with Joseph became one of the ways that God released blessings and favor on Laban's life.

> And Laban said to him, "Please stay, if I have found favor in your eyes, for I have learned by experience that the Lord has blessed me for your sake." Then he said, "Name me your wages, and I will give it." So Jacob said to him, "You know how I have served you and how your livestock has been with me. For what you had before I came was little, and it has increased to a great amount; the Lord has blessed you since my coming. And now, when shall I also provide for my own house?" (Genesis 30:27-30 NKJV)

The scripture above is a biblical example of why your connections are important. Your connections can cause favor to come upon your life. Your connections can cause the winds of favor to blow strongly over your life. Both Laban and Joseph knew that God blessed Laban for Joseph's sake. Joseph reminded Laban thier connection was the reason why Laban increased in a great amount. God wants to release favor over the lives of others for your sake. God wants your life to overflow with favor. The wind of unlimited favor is coming to blow away lack and blow in abundance.

The wind of unlimited favor is coming to blow away poverty and blow in prosperity. The devil wants to place limitation and lack on your life so he attacks your finances and your favor. However, when the wind of unlimited favor blows upon your life you step into the realm of never-ending blessings and you realize that you can experience boundless favor. When the wind of unlimited favor blows upon your life you get the revelation that the favor of God upon your life is inexhaustible. God gives you back what you lost, He restores your blessings and favor.

The wind of unlimited favor is a wind of restoration, it restores the blessings and favor that God originally intended for us to live in. The wind of unlimited favor is coming to restore everything that was taken from you. The winds of favor are blowing because it is restoration time for you. You may have thought you lost the favor of God, but God is about to reinstate His favor in your life. It may seems as if you have lost time, but God is about to redeem the time and restore everything that rightfully belongs to you.

Be glad then, you children of Zion,
And rejoice in the Lord your God;
For He has given you the former rain faithfully,
And He will cause the rain to come down for you—
The former rain,
And the latter rain in the first month.

he threshing floors shall be full of wheat,
And the vats shall overflow with new wine and oil.
"So I will restore to you the years that the swarming locust has
eaten,
The crawling locust,
The consuming locust,
And the chewing locust,
My great army which I sent among you.
You shall eat in plenty and be satisfied,
And praise the name of the Lord your God,
Who has dealt wondrously with you;
And My people shall never be put to shame.
- Joel 2:23-26 (AMP)

The wind of unlimited favor is about to blow over your life and you're not going to lack any good thing (Ps. 34:9.10). Even if God has given you a measure of favor it is time for you to receive more favor, it is time for you to have favor in abundance (Matt. 13:12). Think about how your life would be if you had a tremendous amount of favor upon your life. Take a moment right now and think about it. Write down the thoughts the you had and ask God to give you the favor that you just thought about. After you have written your thoughts and requested the favor you just thought about please recognize this: God can give you a greater level of favor than you think and he can give you more favor that you ask for (Eph. 3:20). As you believe God, watch what happens when the wind of unlimited favor blows.

Prophetic Exhortation & Prophecy:

There is no limit to the ridiculous favor that I am releasing. A lifetime of favor is your portion, not a season says the Lord. Some of you have experienced occasional favor, but I'm taking My righteous ones into a life of consistent favor.

My favor is not like a bank account where sometimes you can't make a withdrawal because the account is empty. My favor does not run empty, no it is never depleted. There is no lack of favor in Me, I am able to release consistent favor into the lives of My people. My favor is boundless and as you consistently pray for Me to release favor into the lives of others you are depositing favor and you will withdraw favor from me says God. Your prayers and decrees are your deposit into your heavenly bank account. Yes, as you sow favor your favor multiplies, it compounds at an accelerated rate. When your earthly bank account is low your heavenly bank account of favor can still reach billionaire status.

I said in My Word that I am able to make ALL GRACE (FAVOR) ABOUND towards you that you may have all sufficiency in all things so that you may have abundance in every good work! My grace, my favor is connected to abundance. You can have favor in all things! Yes, you may have abundance because of My favor.

You cannot exhaust My favor, it is limitless. Your

finances may run low, but your favor can always be in overflow status. This favor will always replenish your finances, but it will also cause you to go to places that your bank account can't get you to.

My unlimited favor can open doors no man can shut. My unlimited favor can not only put you before great men and women of influence, it can make you a great man or woman of influence. My unlimited favor can take you from a low place to a high place. My unlimited favor can take you from the background to the forefront. My unlimited favor can take you from poverty to prosperity. Yes, my unlimited favor can take you from broke to financial breakthrough.

Receive my boundless favor. Receive my unlimited favor. I am ready to release unlimited favor upon your life says the Lord.

- FAVOR MEDITATION -

And God is able to make all grace abound toward you, that you, always having all sufficiency in all things, may have an abundance for every good work.
- 2 Corinthians 9:8

WINDS OF FAVOR

4

FEARLESS FAVOR

According to the word that I covenanted with you when you came out of Egypt, so My Spirit remains among you; do not fear!' - Haggai 2:5 (NKJV)

In Chapter 1 you read how Esther was initially afraid to go before the king. However, after fasting Esther became fearless. After fasting, Esther boldly yet humbly went before the king's throne. As a result of her fearlessness, Esther obtained special favor, a law was ignored for Esther! Instead of being killed, Esther found favor. God revealed to me that Esther experienced "fearless favor". Fearless favor is a result of pressing forward in prayer and fasting to obtain something from God. When you humbly, but boldly go before God's throne of favor something happens - you receive answers to prayer requests that other do not receive and you experience a wind of favor blowing over your life that others do not experience.

There is a special wind of favor, the Wind of "Fearless Favor", that blows upon people that boldly go before the throne of God knowing that the Chief Intercessor, the King of kings goes before us.

Esther is a great biblical example of someone that had "fearless favor" because she boldly went before the king not knowing if she would be sentenced to death or if she would have favor with the king. After 3 days of fasting, Esther may have questioned if she had favor with a natural king, but after seeking God in prayer and fasting Esther knew that she had the favor of God on her life as an orphan-Queen. Just as Esther found favor with the king we have all found favor with the King of kings, Jesus.

Fearless Favor is favor that God puts upon you on greater and greater levels as you seek Him. Fearless favor gives you fearless confidence in God. When God releases a fearless favor upon His people He also releases a fearless confidence at the same time. Is the devil trying to attack your confidence in yourself and in God? If so, you need to go before the throne of grace and ask God to release a new level of fearless favor upon your life. Once you recognize that God has given you fearless favor embrace it and the confidence that comes with it. Don't give your fearless confidence away because it carries "a great and glorious compensation of reward"

Do not, therefore, fling away your fearless confidence, for it carries a great and glorious compensation of reward. - Hebrews 10:35(AMP)

Fearless favor gives you the ability to do the Lord's work. When Esther stood before the king she risked her life to save God's people, she was doing the work of the Lord. Fearless favor is integral to doing the Lord's work.

Paul knew that fearlessness was key to doing the work of the Lord. Paul sent Timothy to see the Corinthians and Paul told the Corinthians to put Timothy at ease so he can fearlessly do the Lord's work among them. Paul fearlessly did the Lord's work so he wanted Timothy to fearlessly do the work just like him. Paul used his fearless favor to influence people to help Timothy in ministry.

When Timothy arrives, see to it that [you put him at ease, so that] he may be fearless among you, for he is [devotedly] doing the Lord's work, just as I am. So [see to it that] no one despises him or treats him as if he were of no account or slights him. But send him off [cordially, speed him on his way] in peace, that he may come to me, for I am expecting him [to come along] with the other brethren. - 1 Corinthians 16:10-11 (AMP)

Fearless favor gives you fearless confidence to do the Lord's work and it gives you protection. The Corinthians were given a command to watch over Timothy; they had to ensure that people treated Timothy properly while he was doing the Lord's work and preparing for his next apostolic assignment. We all need fearless favor. Fearless favor gives you the boldness to do whatever God tells you to do even if there are obstacles or opposition.

> I have great boldness and free and fearless confidence and cheerful courage toward you; my pride in you is great. I am filled [brimful] with the comfort [of it]; with all our tribulation and in spite of it, [I am filled with comfort] I am overflowing with joy.
> (2 Corinthians 7:4 AMP)

God has not given you a spirit of fear (2 Tim. 1:7). There comes a time in your life when you must face your fears and courageously press forward. There is a special wind of favor that comes upon your life when you put your trust in God and fearlessly step out in faith to obey Him.

Prophetic Exhortation & Prophecy:

While on my flight I heard something interesting.....

"Fearless Favor"

The Lord said I'm about to release a fearless favor over my people that will cause them to be bold for Me! They will fear no man!!! This favor causes you to go into the enemy's camp and take what belongs to you! Fearless favor gives you courage and it gives you power from on High!

My fearless favor caused Israel to ask the Egyptians to give them gold, silver & clothing & the Egyptians did it!!!! I gave Israel favor in the sight of the ones that enslaved them and not only did they leave suddenly they left wealthy!!! My people didn't go out scared, they went out bold & they left with a financial breakthrough because of My fearless favor!

My fearless favor is going to cause you to go back to people who told you "no" and they will say "YES"!!!! The devil that stole from you is about vomit up what belongs to you upon your bold command!

My fearless favor caused Esther to proclaim "if i perish, i perish" when she went before the king and could've been put to death. The King couldn't kill her because My fearless favor preserved her life & saved a nation!!!!

My fearless favor is for those that are ready to confront the enemy! My fearless favor is for those ready to face opposition to see the things change for My glory says God! My fearless favor is for those who will cry aloud and spare not! My fearless favor will cause you to roar and nothing will be able to stand against you because I am with you says God! Fearless favor comes straight from my throne and brings your from the background to the forefront despite opposition!!

My fearless favor is about to set My people free!!!! My fearless favor is going to cause you to walk in a new boldness & liberty!!!

- FAVOR MEDITATION -

For God has not given us a spirit of fear, but of power and of love and of a sound mind.
- 2 Tim. 1:7

5

EXPLOSIVE FAVOR

*Suddenly a prophet approached Ahab king of Israel, saying,
"Thus says the Lord: 'Have you seen all this great multitude?
Behold, I will deliver it into your hand today, and you shall know
that I am the Lord.'"
(1 Kings 20:13 NKJV)*

Explosive favor is sudden favor. Explosive favor causes people to suddenly appear in your life to provide prophetic counsel, encouragement, wisdom and support. When the wind of explosive favor blows you recognize that God is with you and that He will move on your behalf. Ahad, king of Israel, was preparing for battle and suddenly a prophet appeared who prophesied victory that very day. The king of Israel experienced "explosive favor"; suddenly he received notice that he was the victor in the battle before the battle started. This reminds me of an old gospel song "Don't wait until the battle is over, shout now. You know in the and you're going to win." Shout now. Your are a winner.

An explosive is a "sudden outburst" so explosive favor is a sudden outburst of favor. God wants you to experience a sudden outburst of favor. An explosive is sparked by something. Humility can spark an outburst of favor. Giving can spark an outburst of favor. Prayer and fasting can spark an outburst of favor. Sowing favor can spark an outburst of favor. Your faithful service to those who have authority over you can spark an outburst of favor. Asking can spark an outburst of favor. Because God is a good God, He can release upon your life explosive favor, that is an outburst of favor, simply because He wants to bless you.

Elisha experienced explosive favor. Elisha faithfully served Elijah. Elisha asked Elijah to do something for him, Elisha wanted favor from Elijah. Elisha asked for a double portion of Elijah's spirit. In response to Elisha's faithfulness and because he asked, Elisha received explosive favor. The wind of explosive favor blew over Elisha's life. Elisha received a sudden outburst of favor. Elisha faithfully served Elijah and he saw the anointing on Elijah's life during his time of service. Elisha wanted a favor, not only did he want the same anointing that Elijah had, he wanted a double portion of Elijah's anointing. If we are honest with ourselves, we can admit that we want the gifts and anointing of our leaders so that we can use them according to how God created us. Elisha received an outburst of favor because he was a faithful servant. Faithful servants are favored servants.

Elisha humbly followed Elijah and I am sure Elisha was secretly saying I want to do the mighty works that my leader , Elijah, does and more. One day Elisha was given an opportunity to ask for the favor he wanted and Elisha's request was granted suddenly. Elijah was suddenly taken away and Elisha suddenly received his request. Elisha's faithful service and bold request caused him to receive explosive favor.

> And so it was, when they had crossed over, that Elijah said to Elisha, "Ask! What may I do for you, before I am taken away from you?" Elisha said, "Please let a double portion of your spirit be upon me." So he said, "You have asked a hard thing. Nevertheless, if you see me when I am taken from you, it shall be so for you; but if not, it shall not be so." Then it happened, as they continued on and talked, that suddenly a chariot of fire appeared with horses of fire, and separated the two of them; and Elijah went up by a whirlwind into heaven. And Elisha saw it, and he cried out, "My father, my father, the chariot of Israel and its horsemen!" So he saw him no more. And he took hold of his own clothes and tore them into two pieces. He also took up the mantle of Elijah that had fallen from him, and went back and stood by the bank of the Jordan. Then he took the mantle of Elijah that had fallen from him, and struck the water, and said, "Where is the Lord God of Elijah?" And when he also had struck the water, it was divided this way and that; and Elisha crossed over. Now when the sons of the prophets who were from Jericho saw him, they said, "The spirit of Elijah rests on

Elisha." And they came to meet him, and
bowed to the ground before him.
(2 Kings 2:9-15 NKJV)

Explosive favor causes a sudden shift in your
situation. However, explosive favor often times comes
after consistent selfless service and patiently waiting on
the Lord. Sudden favor may happen during consistent
prayer, sowing favor and faithful service. Many people
want to receive a "double portion" anointing or they
want the winds of explosive favor to blow over their
lives, but they do not want to pay the price for the
things that they want. Are you one of those people? If
so, consider your ways. Humble yourself before the
Lord and allow God to blow the winds of favor over
your life as you humbly serve. Explosive favor can
suddenly shift you from a low place to a high place,
from the valley to the mountain top, from overlooked to
overbooked, from poverty to prosperity, from lack to
abundance, from just enough to more than enough
from and from a dry land to a land filled with water.

Now it happened in the morning, when the
grain offering was offered, that suddenly
water came by way of Edom, and the land
was filled with water. (2 Kings 3:20 NKJV)

The wind of explosive favor is coming to change
your life. The wind of explosive favor is coming to blow
up the plans and plots of the devil. You have the ability
to position yourself to receive favor. Explosives are
ignited. You can ignite the wind of explosive favor in
your life. You can suddenly experience the winds of
favor suddenly blow in your life.

Prophetic Exhortation & Prophecy:

I was awaken very early this morning for prayer and when praying for God to release favor upon the life of others I heard the word "explosive". God is about to release explosive favor in the lives of some people. I decided to google "explosive favor" and this is the first image I saw.

An explosive is a "sudden outburst"

I am about to release sudden outbursts of favor says the Lord. This favor is going to be released quickly and it's going to be powerful says the Lord. This is that favor that is a force - it has the power to suddenly shift your position from a low place to a high place. This favor is about to come over your life suddenly and it's going to overtake you. This favor is going to cause the Holy Spirit to reignite you and cause the favor of the Most High to overshadow. This favor is going to take you from bondage to breakthrough quickly. Yes, there's about to be an outburst of favor that's causes Me to break out on your behalf so that you experience breakthrough.

This favor is going to destroy every demonic plot and satanic plan attacking your life. This favor releases boldness upon your life. You'll confront unrighteousness and injustice without demonic backlash. This favor open doors for you because of your stance for Me says God. This favor will come upon you so fast that people will be shocked! You're going to be shocked! This sudden outburst of favor is going to shock you. Explosive favor happen in an instant. Yes, it is coming suddenly.

This favor is for the army of God. This favor is for those who declare "the Kingdom of heaven suffers violence and the violent take it by force!" I'm giving you an outburst of favor so that you take what belongs to you. The Lord says My favor is about to cause you to win some spiritual battles. This favor is about to violently effect your enemies! Some of you are stuck fighting for what rightfully belongs to you and this favor is going to result in a supernatural release. My peace belongs to you. My joy belongs to you. The power to get wealth belongs to you. No more blockage and no more delay. You've been waiting for your time and your turn. Well, the Lord said this explosive favor is taking you from next to NOW.

An explosive causes a "rapid change"

This explosive favor is about to cause a rapid change in your life. I see a group of people moving in slow motion; they are dragging in life because it seems there's no way out of certain situations. God said this favor is about to cause a rapid change in circumstances, the plots of enemies of your destiny are about to be destroyed! This favor is about to put you on a fast-track in the spirit and you're about to regain your momentum in the middle of the year. You're about to bust out of your rut. Favor is about to erupt in your life.

This is world-changing favor. This favor happens quickly and it's that favor that ignites you to pray with fervency, decree with authority and causes everything to be destroyed that's in your way. Yes, this favor releases my exousia - that is it releases My power, My strength,

My dominion says God! This explosive favor is coming upon those that want to turn the world upside down! This favor is for the giant slayers, this favor is for the champions, this favor is for the difference makers. This favor comes upon those who favor my righteous causes says the Lord. Because you favor My righteous cause you're about to receive explosive favor in return. Those who favor My righteous cause magnify Me and these are ones that I take pleasure in. Yes, I take pleasure in your prosperity says the Lord. My explosive favor is coming upon those that take a stance for me and prosperity is released with it. Get ready for My explosive favor!

- FAVOR MEDITATION -

And suddenly a voice came from heaven, saying, "This is My beloved Son, in whom I am well pleased."
- Matthew 3:7

6

DELUGE OF FAVOR

As I was writing this book I heard the Lord say "I want to overwhelm My people with favor. I want them to experience a flood of favor. I am about to inundate My people with favor and they will know that I AM that I AM." I encourage you to make this simple, but powerful declaration:

> "I am experiencing a flood of favor. God daily floods me with favor. Everywhere I go, God is drenching me with favor. I am overwhelmed by the favor of God on my life."

When the winds of favor blow powerfully you will experience a deluge of favor. When winds blow they can be soft winds or strong winds. The stronger the wind the more powerful the wind. A soft wind is like a cool summer breeze in California, but a powerful wind is like the winds in the city of my hometown Chicago, the "Windy City". When God told me that the winds of favor are blowing and I heard the phrase "deluge of favor". The word "deluge" is defined as follows:

> "a great flood of water; inundation; flood; a drenching rain; downpour; .anything that overwhelms like a flood:"

I immediately thought of winds so strong that it would move you and overwhelm you. I thought about my numerous experiences being in the midst of the Chicago winds. Chicago winds move you, they push you and they do not let you stay in the same place or move at the same speed. Chicago winds inundate you and overwhelm you, but there are other places in the world that have stronger winds than Chicago. If strong winds are near water the winds move the water. The winds' movement of the water can be so strong that the water will flood locations. Strong winds inundate entire cities and regions. God used the natural description of winds blowing as a prophetic picture of what happens when God blows His strong winds of favor. God strong winds of favor cause a deluge of favor.

Although I mentioned it in this book already, a scripture that aligns with the definition of deluge is Joel 2:23-27. In Job Chapter 2, God released a deluge of favor and the children of Zion experienced the following things:

- God's faithful release of rain, His blessings;

- A double portion of blessings; God

release the former rain and latter rain at the same time;

— No lack; God ensures that your needs are met;

— An overflow of new things; God moves you out of old experiences and gives you new ones;

— Supernatural restoration; God takes inventory of things that were taken from you and gives them back to you;

— The divine protection of God; God sends a host of angels to watch over you and protect you;

— More than enough; God gives you plenty and make sure that you are satisfied;

— Protection of your character; God ensures that shame does not come upon your name; and

— The presence of God in your life; God stays in your midst and He does things so you will know He alone is God.

A deluge of favor causes great winds of favor to strongly blow in your life causing you to experience Joel 2:23-27

Be glad then, you children of Zion,
And rejoice in the Lord your God;
For He has given you the former rain faithfully,
And He will cause the rain to come down for you—
The former rain,

And the latter rain in the first month.
The threshing floors shall be full of wheat,
And the vats shall overflow with new wine and oil.
"So I will restore to you the years that the swarming locust has
eaten,
The crawling locust,
The consuming locust,
And the chewing locust,
My great army which I sent among you.
You shall eat in plenty and be satisfied,
And praise the name of the Lord your God,
Who has dealt wondrously with you;
And My people shall never be put to shame.
Then you shall know that I am in the midst of Israel:
I am the Lord your God
And there is no other.
My people shall never be put to shame.
Joel 2:23-27(AMP)

There are times in life when you need to experience a deluge of favor. To receive a deluge of favor you must first be thankful for the measure of favor that you have or that God gives to you. You must be faithful to God in the little things that He gives you in order to receive more. Be grateful for small favor and you'll get more favor.

God wants to give you more favor, He wants you to experience a deluge of favor. A deluge of favor is when God opens the flood gates of Heaven (Mal. 3:10). In Malachi Chapter 3, faithful tithing and giving are the prerequisites for the flood gates of Heaven to be open and to receive an outpouring of blessings. Do not let people discourage you from obeying God and spending significant time in His presence because your diligence may be the determining factor for the release of a deluge of favor.

Prophetic Exhortation & Prophecy:

I just ended a periscope of suddenly decrees & favor confessions and the Lord gave me "deluge of favor"

Because of your focus and leap of faith some of you will experience a deluge of favor! You are about to be inundated with a great quantity of favor. My favor is about to bombard you says God!

This deluge of favor will cause the wealth of the wicked to be transferred into the lives of the just suddenly. This favor makes you a money magnet. Start those business and step out in purpose, My deluge of favor will catapult you!

This deluge of favor is about to drench you! Yes, a tsunami of favor is about to hit you!!!! Favor is about to rush towards you and pour out over you!

Get ready for a deluge of favor! My people will experience an influx of favor. As you enter into a new month you're entering in with a new level of favor. Continue to confess that you walk in My favor. Continue to humbly come before my throne of favor! Massive favor is your portion! A deluge of favor is rushing your way!

- FAVOR MEDITATION -

And God is able to make all grace [every favor and earthly blessing] come in abundance to you, so that you may always [under all circumstances, regardless of the need] have complete sufficiency in everything [being completely self-sufficient in Him], and have an abundance for every good work and act of charity. 1 2 Cor. 9:8(AMP)

7

FINANCIAL FAVOR

Blessed and fortunate and happy and spiritually prosperous (in that state in which the born-again child of God enjoys His favor and salvation) are those who hunger and thirst for righteousness (uprightness and right standing with God), for they shall be completely satisfied! - Mathew 5:6 (AMP)

The will of God is for His children to be prosperous in every area of life. Financial favor is the type of favor that breaks financial bondage and ushers in financial breakthrough. When the wind of financial favor blows your financial situation is transformed. The wind of financial transformation will cause the following to occur:

- unexpected checks in the mail;

- sudden deposits in your online accounts;

- double and triple your fee for products &

services:

- unimagined financial support;
- sudden financial increase;
- unanticipated vision investors;
- invitations & plane tickets;
- gifts & surprises; and
- so much more.

Israel experienced the winds of financial favor when they left Egypt. God acted on Israel's behalf when He set them free physically and financially. God told Israel that they would not leave their season of bondage empty handed; the Egyptians (the very people that held them in captivity) would release wealth to them. The winds of financial favor blew and wealth came. God gave Israel favor with the Egyptians and the entire nation went from bondage to financial breakthrough.

> And I will give this people favor in the sight of the Egyptians; and it shall be, when you go, that you shall not go empty-handed. But every woman shall ask of her neighbor, namely, of her who dwells near her house, articles of silver, articles of gold, and clothing; and you shall put them on your sons and on your daughters. So you shall plunder the Egyptians." - Exodus 3:21,22 (NKJV)

You may feel as if your life has been marked for a lifetime of bondage, but when the wind of financial favor blows in your life you will experience sudden financial freedom. Chains of financial bondage will be broken off of your life suddenly. Your days of financial lack are coming to an end. The winds of financial favor are going to blow in your financial supporters, your Kingdom connections and your marketplace partners. The winds of financial favor will cause money to come into your life in ways that will shock you. Often times I read ads on social media and I see people chasing money. However, God did not create us to chase wealth. God wants us to pursue vision and money will come to us. God wants us to seek first the Kingdom of God and then watch the wind of financial favor blow in our lives. God wants to take whatever we have, blow on it, multiply it and shift our financial situations just like He did with the indebted widow/single mom who asked Elisha for help.

> A certain woman of the wives of the sons of the prophets cried out to Elisha, saying, "Your servant my husband is dead, and you know that your servant feared the Lord. And the creditor is coming to take my two sons to be his slaves." So Elisha said to her, "What shall I do for you? Tell me, what do you have in the house?" And she said, "Your maidservant has nothing in the house but a jar of oil." Then he said, "Go, borrow vessels from everywhere, from all your neighbors— empty vessels; do not gather just a few. And when you have come in, you shall shut the door behind you and your sons; then pour it into all those vessels, and set aside the full ones." So she went from him and shut the door behind her and her sons, who brought

the vessels to her; and she poured it out. Now it came to pass, when the vessels were full, that she said to her son, "Bring me another vessel." And he said to her, "There is not another vessel." So the oil ceased. Then she came and told the man of God. And he said, "Go, sell the oil and pay your debt; and you and your sons live on the rest." 2 Kings 4:1-7(NKJV)

Ask God to blow the wind of financial favor over your life. You have not because you ask not. Don't ask for a small amount of financial favor ask God to release a large amount of financial favor, a level of favor so great that your financial situation changes supernaturally and suddenly. Ecclesiastes 10:19 says that "...money answers everything." so do not let the devil trick you into thinking you must take a vow of poverty to prove that you are a submitted Saint of God. Jesus became poor so that through His poverty you might become rich (2 Cor. 8:9). Tell God your financial situation and pray for the wind of favor to blow over your life.

> "Ask, and it will be given to you; seek, and you will find; knock, and it will be opened to you." -*Matthew 7:7 (NKJV)*

The widow saw Elisha and she was not afraid to tell the prophet of God her situation; she was not hesitant to ask for instructions to fix her situation. You must not only tell God your financial situation, you must request instructions to fix your situation. You must linger in God's presence until you receive an answer. If you are in debt, if you are trying to make ends meet, if you are robbing Peter to pay Paul, if you are living from check to check, or if you are living off just enough, you are a candidate for financial favor. If the above descriptions describes your life, you need the wind of financial favor to blow. If you do not have the financial resources to see your visions and dreams become a reality, you are a candidate for financial favor. If your income is low or if you are not experiencing a consistent increase in your income, you are a candidate for financial favor. God does not want you to live in lack. God wants the wind of financial favor to blow in your life because He takes pleasure in the prosperity of His servants.

> Let them shout for joy and be glad, Who favor my righteous cause; And let them say continually, "Let the Lord be magnified, Who has pleasure in the prosperity of His servant." - *Ps. 35:27(NKJV)*

Take inventory of your life. Are you humble? Are you a servant of God? Do you favor the righteous causes of God? If you answered "yes" to these questions, God wants to take pleasure in you so He is releasing a fresh wind of financial favor over your life. Some of you reading this book are questioning the release of this wind of financial favor because generations of your family have lived in poverty. As you are reading this chapter you might be thinking about how you have been trying to get a financial breakthrough for a long time. If you are reading this chapter and you have questions about how God can transform your financial situation, answer this question:

Is there anything too hard for God?

God is able to do exceedingly abundantly above what you ask or think (Ephesians 3:20)! It is not too hard for God to blow the wind of financial favor over your life. It is not too hard for God to raise you up to be the bloodline breaker of financial distress in your family. God can raise you up to be the person in your family that breaks the cycle of poverty and lack. The wind of financial favor destroys debt and place upon you an anointing that makes you a money magnet. God's wind of financial favor takes you into your wealthy place.

> Thou hast caused men to ride over our heads; we went through fire and through water: but thou broughtest us out into a wealthy place. - Psalms 66:12

God wants to bring you out of your current financial stress and into a wealthy place. A wealthy place is a place of favor and blessings. As mentioned in prior chapters, you can position yourself for favor. One of the ways that you can position yourself for the wind of financial favor to blow in your life is by sowing. God is putting an Issac anointing on His people. Issac sowed and he reaped favor and blessings.

Issac positioned himself for the wind of financial favor to blow in his life by sowing. As a result of Issac's sowing, he reaped a one-hundred fold return. Issac sowed his finances and he received an outpour of financial favor.

> Then Isaac sowed in that land, and received in the same year an hundredfold: and the Lord blessed him. - Gen. 26:12

The wind of financial favor blew so strongly in Issac's life that the following things happened:

- The Lord favored him with blessings;

- He became a great man;

- He gained more and more;

- He became very wealthy; and

- He became very distinguished.

> Then Isaac planted [seed] in that land [as a farmer] and reaped in the same year a hundred times [as much as he had planted], and the Lord blessed and favored him. And the man [Isaac] became great and gained more and more until he became very wealthy and extremely distinguished; he owned flocks and herds and a great household [with a number of servants], and the Philistines envied him. - Genesis 26:12-14

If you read the above scriptures out of context you may assume that the everything was going great for Issac and around Issac. However, the assumption would be inaccurate. Everything was not great around Issac; there was a famine in the land. In the midst of famine God gave Issac some simple instructions, go where I tell you to go and I will bless you. Further, God told Issac that He would carry out the oath He swore to Abraham if Issac was obedient. In other words, Issac was also receiving favor and blessings because of Abraham. You are descendant of Abraham just like Issac and you are entitled to blessings and favor of Abraham just like Issac as long as you obey God.

You are the sons (descendants) of the prophets and [heirs] of the covenant which God made with your fathers, saying to Abraham, 'And in your seed (descendant) all the families of the earth shall be blessed. - Acts 3:25 (AMP)

The wind of financial favor is going to blow strongly over the lives of those individuals that obey God. Ask God for favor. Pray for your needs and the needs of others. Humbly go before God's throne of favor and watch the winds of favor blow over your life.

Prayer:

Father God, I come before your throne of favor and I ask you to give [us] [we] *me what I need. Activate the power to get wealth that's on the inside of* [us] [us] [our] [us] *me. Help me to be a wise steward over my finances, Lord. Give me* [we] [we are] *discipline to give generously so that I may reap abundantly. I am a* [we] [us] *descendent of Abraham and I humbly ask you to bless me with the* [us] *blessings that you promised Abraham. Give me treasures of darkness* [us] *and hidden riches in secret places. Make me a money magnet, touch the* [us] *hearts of people and ignite them to bless me, Blow Your wind of* [our] [lives] *financial favor over my life.*

Prophetic Exhortation & Prophecy:

And when I was with you and ran short financially, I did not burden any [of you], for what I lacked was abundantly made up by the brethren who came from Macedonia. So I kept myself from being burdensome to you in any way, and will continue to keep [myself from being so]. - 2 Corinthians 11:9(AMP)

Financial favor is about to show up in your situation! Debts are being cancelled, lost money will be found & money is coming your way because of your labor. This is not a reference to physical labor, but years you spent laboring in fasting and prayers. You're about to reap financial favor because you sowed sacrificially and gave until it hurt! Oh yes, a supernatural transfer is about to take place. Financial favor is on its way. Wealth is being transferred into your hands. I'm releasing financial favor that others will see, but not understand.

Money cometh says God! Money cometh right your way - it's breakthrough time.....no more delay. This financial favor is about to usher you into your wealthy place. I said I take pleasure in the prosperity of my servant. It is my pleasure to release financial favor into the lives of my servants.

Jesus became poor so that you may become rich. Yes, Jesus became poor so that through His poverty you may be rich - that you may have financial favor! It is not my will for you to be weighed down with money problems! My will is for you to be financially free. This financial favor is going to liberate you. I'm about to bless you so that you will be a blessing. Financial favor is coming to you so I can use you as a vessel to release financial favor says the Lord.

This financial favor will make you a money magnet. Blessings are about to pursue you and overtake you suddenly. You thought you needed more work to have more money, but you need is more favor says the Lord. You need financial favor and it is indeed coming your way. It will not delay. Financial favor is coming your way!

- FAVOR MEDITATION -

Now there was a famine in the land [of Canaan], besides the previous famine that had occurred in the days of Abraham. So Isaac went to Gerar, to Abimelech king of the Philistines. The Lord appeared to him and said, "Do not go down to Egypt; stay in the land of which I will tell you. Live temporarily [as a resident] in this land and I will be with you and will bless and favor you, for I will give all these lands to you and to your descendants, and I will establish and carry out the oath which I swore to Abraham your father. I will make your descendants multiply as the stars of the heavens, and will give to your descendants all these lands; and by your descendants shall all the nations of the earth be blessed, because Abraham listened to and obeyed My voice and [consistently] kept My charge, My commandments, My statutes, and My laws."
- Genesis 26:1-5

8

EXTRAVAGANT FAVOR

So when the king's command and his decree were proclaimed and when many maidens were gathered in Shushan the capital under the custody of Hegai, Esther also was taken to the king's house into the custody of Hegai, keeper of the women. And the maiden pleased [Hegai] and obtained his favor. And he speedily gave her the things for her purification and her portion of food and the seven chosen maids to be given her from the king's palace; and he removed her and her maids to the best [apartment] in the harem. (Esther 2:8-9 AMP)

Do you know that the favor of God will cause you to live an extravagant life? I know many people have been told that the poor are blessed, but there are many ways to receive the blessings of God. In fact, according to 2 Corinthians 8:9, Jesus became poor so that through

His poverty we may become rich. God does not want everyone to be poor and this is evident because Jesus became poor that we may be rich. The wind of extravagant favor blew over Esther's life. Esther found favor in the sight of Hegai, the king's eunuch, and she experienced the best (Esther 2:9-10). God gave Esther favor with someone that could help her prepare and position herself for a greater level of favor. Hegai introduced this orphan girl to the finer things of life and it was only the beginning. As queen, Esther would receive so much more favor because she listened to Hegai. I am sure all of the women that were gathered in Shushan for preparation to meet the king all had comfortable and beautiful places to reside during the preparation and waiting process. Esther, however, received favor and she resided in the best living quarters available along with her seven maidens. God wants you to experience the best just like Esther.

> And Pharaoh said to Joseph, Tell your brothers this: Load your animals and return to the land of Canaan, And get your father and your households and come to me. And I will give you the best in the land of Egypt and you will live on the fat of the land. You therefore command them, saying, You do this: take wagons from the land of Egypt for your little ones and for your wives, and bring your father and come. Also do not look with regret or concern upon your goods, for the best of all the land of Egypt is yours. (Genesis 45:17-20 NKJV)

The wind of extravagant favor blew over Esther's life and she received the best among women. In the same manner, the window of extravagant favor blew over Joseph's life and he stood out among his siblings from the time he was a child. Although Joseph experienced tragedies in life he eventually experienced the best of a nation.

Joseph was told that the best of all the land of Egypt was his. Can you imagine being told that the best of what's available belongs to you? Joseph was told that he would have the fat (wealth) of the land. Pharaoh, a pagan ruler, saw the favor on Joseph's life so he was ready and willing to invest in Joseph's wisdom. In my over 20 years of salvation I have heard people pray for the treasures of darkness and hidden riches (Isaiah 45:4), but many of these same people are too religious to advise a modern day pharaoh. Some people miss their investors because God has stirred the spirit of a non-Christian leader to give them hidden riches, but they will not accept them because that person is not a Christian. God spoke to Cyrus, the king of Persia, and commanded him to build a house for him even though he was not part of God's chosen nation. God stirred up Cyrus and Cyrus gave the best of all that he possessed for the building of the Lord's house.

> Now in the first year of Cyrus king of Persia, that the word of the Lord by the mouth of Jeremiah might be fulfilled, the Lord stirred up the spirit of Cyrus king of Persia, so that he made a proclamation throughout all his kingdom, and also put it in writing, saying, Thus says Cyrus king of Persia: All the

kingdoms of the earth the Lord God of heaven has given me. And He has commanded me to build Him a house at Jerusalem which is in Judah. Who is among you of all His people? May the Lord his God be with him, and let him go up! (2 Chronicles 36:22-23)

The people of God could have rejected God's help through Cyrus because of the person that he used, but they did not. A religious mindset will result in the winds of favor blowing pass you. The winds of favor did not pass by Joseph, he advised pharaoh and he received the best. Be open to the wind of favor blowing over your life in unique ways. If you want the winds of favor to blow over your life you must allow the wind to blow God's way even if that means accepting financial blessings from someone outside of your religious circle.

The anointing on Joseph'a life opened a door for him to help governmental, societal and business leaders and in return not only did he receive an overflow of blessings but he also helped God's people. When the wind of extravagant favor blow in your life the blessings you receive could come from anyone at anytime, but you must remember a day will come when you must help the Saints of the Most High God. The wind of extravagant favor does not blow over your life just for you; you must release favor to someone else.

Again, humility is a key way to position yourself for the winds of favor to blow over your life, especially the wind of extravagant favor. God gives grace (favor) to the humble (James 4:6). Because of your humility, the winds of extravagant favor can blow over your life even when you don't think that you deserve. The prodigal son returned home believing that he was not even worthy to be recognized. However, his father (just like our Heavenly Father) believed that he was deserving of the best.

> And the son said to him, Father, I have sinned against heaven and in your sight; I am no longer worthy to be called your son [I no longer deserve to be recognized as a son of yours]! But the father said to his bond servants, bring quickly the best robe (the festive robe of honor) and put it on him; and give him a ring for his hand and sandals for his feet. And bring out that [wheat-] fattened calf and kill it; and let us revel and feast and be happy and make merry, because this my son was dead and is alive again; he was lost and is found! And they began to revel and feast and make merry. (Luke 15:21-24)

You may believe that you have lost your ability to go before the throne of grace (favor). You may think because you did not grow up in the perfect biblical settings or because you made some mistakes you cannot go before the King and make a request. Do not let your heart condemn you because if your heart does not condemn you, you can have confidence towards God (1 John 3:21).

Esther was an orphan, her uncle was taking caring of her, but she found herself in a position to marry the king and eventually had to go before the king when her action was considered improper. However, Esther had favor throughout the entire process. Esther went into the king's presence because God was with her and she experienced the wind of extravagant favor blow over your life. The prodigal son wasted livelihood and his life became so bad that he was about to eat slop with swine. However, he considered his ways and went back to his father. The prodigal son was not shunned or condemned, he was greeted with love and compassion. The prodigal son made foolish decisions, but he humbled himself and experienced the winds of favor, including extravagant favor, blow over his life. Today, humbly go before the throne of God and ask him to cause the winds of favor to blow over your life.

Prophetic Exhortation & Prophecy:

While in prayer this morning I kept hearing "extravagant"! Extravagant is more than usual, necessary or proper.

God's chosen people will walk in extravagant favor. There is a dimension of favor coming upon the chosen that will cause people to experience the finer things of life, it will put you in the best position and give you access to things average thinking people will not have access to. Extravagant favor is for those handpicked by God. When you cried out to me, when you made sacrifices for Me, when you stood for My righteous causes people said it don't take all that. You chose to please Me, not people says the Lord and in this season of your life I am doing something special for you. I am doing something special for my chosen ones. Yes, many are called and those who are called receive great things and they may even receive the best of things. However, few are chosen. My chosen receives the best of the best says God.

Get ready to go to the best places. Get ready for some of the best experiences that life has to offer. Get ready to be seen as above average. I am about to call my chosen ones out and hand pick them to receive My ultimate best. Yes, some believe that extravagant people are wasteful and unreasonable. However, the Lord says you cannot waste my favor because I have more than enough. I desire to have you walk in a dimension of favor that seems unreasonable - if it was reasonable and rational, it would be limited. This favor is for those that have taken the limits off their minds and Me; they know that they are worthy to receive the best that the world has to offer.

I am releasing extravagant favor upon my humble servants, ones who will not get puffed up when I change their status. Yes, this Favor will look absurd to some and outrageous to others - that's exactly what I release upon my chosen: absurd and outrageous levels of favor! Don't let ordinary minds keep you from experiencing My extraordinary Favor says God. Whoever told you that you were not worthy of the best and most luxurious things in life lied to you. Didn't I say the silver is mine and the gold is mine - all precious metals, jewels and stones are My handiwork and I hand it over to whomever I please says the Lord. My chosen have found favor in My sight because they humble themselves before My throne of grace (favor). I can trust My chosen with the best of the best.

Esther received the best of the best among women. Solomon receive wisdom and wealth unmatched by men. Among his brothers David was chosen as king. Mary was highly favored. Only Joseph had a coat of many colors. These things may have seemed unusual to the people around them, but I do unusual things to confound the minds of men. I am the God of the unusual. I am releasing unusual and extravagant favor.

I am about to work a work in your days that you would not believe though it be told to you. Yes, I'm about to release such extravagant favor on your life that even though you've been believing for favor and praying for favor- it will still be much more than you expected or could even imagine.

My chosen will receive extravagant favor. Don't apologize for this extravagant favor says God. You have laid down your life. Your soul has made its boast in Me says God. You seek no glory for yourself; you let Me use you to draw people to Me. You are the righteousness of God, you are in right standing with Me says the Lord. There is a reward for the righteous. I prepare a table before you in the presence of your enemies, I anoint you, I cause blessings to run over in your life - your cup runs over. Yes, you are properly positioned for the overflow. Yes, you will experience My goodness in the land of the living. You will receive extravagant favor.

- FAVOR MEDITATION -

For You, O Lord, will bless the righteous;
With favor You will surround him as with a shield.
Psalms 5:12 (NKJV)

9

EXTREME FAVOR

The amazement was extreme. "He succeeds in everything he
attempts," they exclaimed; "he even makes deaf men hear and
dumb men speak!"
- Mark 7:37 (WEY)

Extreme favor has extreme results.; it is favor on
steroids. When people see extreme favor operating in
your life they are extremely amazed. God wants the
favor on your life to be so extreme that you can ask for
things and you will get it. The winds of favor can cause
a favor on your life to be so extraordinary that people
will be amazed by the level of favor on your life. God
wants to bless you. God wants to counsel you. God
wants you to seek first the Kingdom of God and all
that you need will be added to you (Matthew 6:33). God
wants the favor on your life to be so great that
everything you do prospers.

Blessed is the man
Who walks not in the counsel of the ungodly,
Nor stands in the path of sinners,
Nor sits in the seat of the scornful;
But his delight is in the law of the Lord,
And in His law he meditates day and night.
He shall be like a tree
Planted by the rivers of water,
That brings forth its fruit in its season,
Whose leaf also shall not wither;
And whatever he does shall prosper.
-Psalms 1:1-3 (NKJV)

Have you ever witnessed a level of favor so great on someone's life that you are amazed? Well, I know one person in the bible that had extreme favor and that was Mary, the mother of Jesus. Mary was blessed and highly favored. To be chosen by God for a special assignment that only you can accomplish is an extreme privilege and that privilege is coupled with extreme favor.

The word "extreme" is defined as reaching a high or highest degree. farthest removed from ordinary or average; utmost; exceedingly great in degree. God wants you to experience very great favor. God wants you to receive the highest level of favor that He has available for you. It is time for you to experience favor. The winds of favor are about to blow over your life and you will experience exceptional favor. "It is time for you to declare that I have extraordinary favor because the wind of extreme favor is blowing over my life", says the Lord.

Are you ready to receive extreme favor? I hope so because God is ready to give it to you. God doesn't want us to have common and ordinary experiences in life, God wants us to have uncommon and extraordinary experiences. God is a specialist in doing more than what we could ever conceive in our minds. God is able to do exceedingly abundantly above all that we ask or think.

> Now to Him who is able to do exceedingly abundantly above all that we ask or think, according to the power that works in us. - Ephesians 3:20 (NKJV)

Please take a moment and think about a life full tremendous favor and consider the biggest favor you could ask someone; God can do exceedingly and abundantly above that thought. Extraordinary favor is the kind of favor that takes you into the realm of experiencing exceedingly and abundantly above all you can ask or think. God is a giver of extreme favor. One of the greatest examples of God blowing a wind of extreme favor is the life of Mary.

Mary had "extreme favor", she was blessed and HIGHLY favored. Others received favor in the bible, but the favor on Mary'a life was very great, it was extraordinary and it was exceptional. Mary could not have thought of being the mother of the Savior of the world. Mary was "highly favored" among all women because she was blessed to do something that no other woman in the world would ever do; give birth to the Messiah. God wants you to be a highly favored person and He wants His people to be highly favored people.

God has called each of us to give birth to something while we are on this earth that no one else in the world can do.

> "Now in the sixth month the angel Gabriel was sent by God to a city of Galilee named Nazareth, to a virgin betrothed to a man whose name was Joseph, of the house of David. The virgin's name was Mary. And having come in, the angel said to her, "Rejoice, highly favored one, the Lord is with you; blessed are you among women!" -Luke 1:26-28 (NKJV)

Mary has extreme favor, the favor on her life was exceedingly great. Israel was a nation that had extreme favor. The Israelites were God's people in the Old Testament and today we are God's people.

> And I will stretch out my hand, and smite Egypt with all my wonders which I will do in the midst thereof: and after that he will let you go. And I will give this people favour in the sight of the Egyptians: and it shall come to pass, that, when ye go, ye shall not go empty. But every woman shall borrow of her neighbour, and of her that sojourneth in her house, jewels of silver, and jewels of gold, and raiment: and ye shall put them upon your sons, and upon your daughters; and ye shall spoil the Egyptians. - Exodus 3:20-22

The Israelites had extreme favor, the Israelites asked a nation of people to give them silver, gold and clothing and received what they requested. God gave the Israelites favor with the Egyptians. God wants to give entire churches extreme favor just like He gave Israel. God wants the wind of favor to blow over your life. God even wants the winds of favor to blow over your ministry and your congregation.

Extreme favor causes supernatural church growth. Extreme favor causes extreme giving to occur in churches. Extreme favor causes people to live under the glory of God for extensive times periods thus resulting in miracles, signs and wonders. The world says you can have a piece of the pie, but there is no limit in God, God can give you the entire pie and just make more pies for other people. Believe God for extreme favor and watch God do extraordinary things in your life.

Prophetic Exhortation & Prophecy:

I recall being young in the Lord and after I read this scripture I would say "I am blessed and highly favored." I was rebuked and told I could not be blessed and highly favored, only Mary could be. I recall saying the bible didn't say no one else could be blessed and "highly favored"   . I was told I should not say that.

Me: (softly responding: "I'm blessed & highly favored")

Sometimes you have to declare things that people don't understand or agree with! We may not receive the same favor as Mary, but we can receive extreme & extraordinary favor. With God, nothing will be impossible!

Decree: God will give me EXTREME favor. I am blessed and HIGHLY favored!

- FAVOR MEDITATION -

After these things the word of the Lord came to Abram in a vision, saying, "Do not be afraid, Abram. I am your shield, your exceedingly great reward."
- Genesis 15:1 (NKJV)

10

JUDGMENT IN YOUR FAVOR

*So shall you find favor, good understanding, and high esteem in
the sight [or judgment] of God and man.*
- Proverbs 3:4 (AMP)

The favor of God causes situations to change in
your favor. There are some situations in our lives that
require divine intervention for them to be fixed. Many
of us think that the judgment of man determines our
fate. However, when God's favor is upon your life
things intended to harm you will turn around for your
good. Merriam-Webtster's Dictionary defines
"judgment"as follows:

> 1.a :the process of forming an opinion or
> evaluation by discerning and comparing
> careful judgment of the odds. b :an opinion

or estimate so formed is not worth doing in my judgment. 2. a :the capacity for judging :discernment be guided by your own judgment showing poor judgment. b :the exercise of this capacity a situation requiring careful judgment. 3. a :a formal utterance of an authoritative opinion. b :an opinion so pronounced. 4. a :a formal decision given by a court. b (1) :an obligation (such as a debt) created by the decree of a court (2) :a certificate evidencing such a decree. 5. a. the final judging of humankind by God sinners awaiting Judgment. b :a divine sentence or decision; specifically :a calamity held to be sent by God believed their bad luck to be a judgment upon them

Judgment already has been made in favor of the Saints of God in the spirit realm. God has already rendered a decision in your favor in the Courts of Heaven. You have already prevailed over every demonic force that is attempting to hold you captive.

> I beheld, and the same horn made war with the saints, and prevailed against them; Until the Ancient of days came, and judgment was given to the saints of the most High; and the time came that the saints possessed the kingdom. - Daniel 7:21,22

The favor of God causes judgments to made in your best interest. Man may have an opinion of you, but God has the final say. It is God that concludes a matter.

> Many seek the ruler's favor, But justice for man comes from the Lord. - Proverbs 29:26

Have you ever been before a judge in court or known someone that has? I am sure that you have. Well, some of you are crying out for a natural judge (a man or woman) to give you justice just like the widow in Luke Chapter 18.

> And he spake a parable unto them to this end, that men ought always to pray, and not to faint; Saying, There was in a city a judge, which feared not God, neither regarded man: And there was a widow in that city; and she came unto him, saying, Avenge me of mine adversary. And he would not for a while: but afterward he said within himself, Though I fear not God, nor regard man; Yet because this widow troubleth me, I will avenge her, lest by her continual coming she weary me. And the Lord said, Hear what the unjust judge saith. And shall not God avenge his own elect, which cry day and night unto him, though he bear long with them? I tell you that he will avenge them speedily. Nevertheless when the Son of man cometh, shall he find faith on the earth? - Luke 18:1-8

Because I am a lawyer, I have gathered information to present to judges and I have seen judges make judicial decisions numerous times. In a courtroom a judge gathers all of the facts and renders a decision. However, God's decision concerning a matter can change the outcome of a legal case. A relationship with God can cause judgments to be made in your favor and prayer can reverse unrighteous judgements made by men and women. God has the heart of kings (people of authority). When you pray God can turn the heart of someone to make a judgment in your favor (Proverbs 21:1).

Has someone made an unfair and uninformed judgment about you or your life? In life, people misjudge others or they have opinions about others based on what people have said instead of based on what God reveals to them. Righteousness and justice are more acceptable to God than sacrifice (Proverbs 21:3). God can correct people's misjudgments about others. God can reveal His opinion about you and it will change people's opinion about you. Don't be overwhelmed by the judgment of men, position yourself before God's presence and He will cause judgments to be made in your favor or turn them around for your favor.

Studying the Bible and living a righteous life are keys to obtaining favor. When God's favor is upon your life, you are held in high esteem in the judgement of man. There are times in our life when it seems as if we are judged unfairly. There are times in life when judgements have to be made and they are not made in our favor. Many times in life people are misjudged or a judgement call is made without all of the facts. God's favor is about to cause a divine reversal in your life. As I was writing this chapter I heard God say that unjust judgments are being reversed. God also said that some people that are awaiting judgment on matters will see the winds of favor blow and judgment will be rendered in their favor. Those who trust in the Lord and pray will see the Lord move on their behalf. The winds of favor our blowing in the lives of those individuals who put their trust in the Lord. Do not put your trust in man, trust God (Isaiah 50:8-10). Trust God; He'll favor you.

Prophetic Exhortation & Prophecy:

You may have entered this month thinking judgment will be made against you. It seems as if the enemy is making war with you and prevailing. Well, the battle is not over and you're about to see victory! satan the accuser of the brethren have tried to rise up against you, but I saw satan fall like lightening. Pride and pompous people seem to be getting ahead, do not be concerned for I resists the proud and gives grace (favor) to the humble says the Lord. Because you continued to walk in humility in times of adversity, a new level of favor is going to fall on your life.

This new level of favor will activate divine reversals in your life. Things that seemed to be going against you will suddenly turnaround in your favor. I'm about to show up as the righteous judge on your behalf and the case the enemy has presented about you is about to settle in your favor. I'm coming as the Ancient of Days and I'm about deal with your enemy and make judgement in your favor. Yes, the Ancient of Days has made and continues to make judgment in favor of the Saints.

So, My people keep doing good for good things are coming your way. Keep sowing because you're about to reap abundantly. Showing kindness and favor towards your enemy is heaping coals on the enemy's head. A great reward is coming to you for showing kindness and consideration towards those that seem unworthy. God said obey Me, bless whom I say bless, show favor to whom I say show favor to for I have a reward to give you for your obedience. That reward is a greater measure of favor. The reward is exponential favor. The reward is supernatural favor.

Fret not for evildoers because they shall be cut down. I know you have had nights of weeping, but my joy is coming your way. My favor brings joy. My joy gives you strength to keep pressing forward. Keep pressing forward despite the tears because I'm about to show up. Yes, I'm showing up as the Ancient of Days and judgment will be made in your favor and you will possess your possessions. You will receive what belongs to you; everything that the thief has taken will be restore sevenfold. You are about to reap a harvest of favor. Judgment is being made in your favor, it is now a time of reaping and restoration. It's time for you to experience My goodness in the land of the living. It's time for you to experience a life of favor.

- FAVOR MEDITATION -

"...and a judgment was made in favor of the saints of the Most High, and the time came for the saints to possess the kingdom."
- Daniel 7:22

11

MIRACULOUS FAVOR

*And the Lord spake unto Moses and unto Aaron, saying,
When Pharaoh shall speak unto you, saying, Shew a miracle for
you: then thou shalt say unto Aaron, Take thy rod, and cast it
before Pharaoh, and it shall become a serpent. And Moses and
Aaron went in unto Pharaoh, and they did so as the Lord had
commanded: and Aaron cast down his rod before Pharaoh, and
before his servants, and it became a serpent. Then Pharaoh also
called the wise men and the sorcerers: now the magicians of
Egypt, they also did in like manner with their enchantments. For
they cast down every man his rod, and they became serpents: but
Aaron's rod swallowed up their rods.
- Exodus 7:8-10*

Favor and miracles flow together. Miraculous favor
will demonstrate to people that God is with you. The
wind of miraculous favor is about to shift your life from

the natural to the supernatural. God's miraculous favor does things that are unusual; it releases His phenomenons. When you have miraculous favor, God does things in your life confounds the minds of men.

When you have favor with God and favor with man there is no circumstances that God cannot turn around for your good. Miraculous favor causes things that appear impossible to become possible. God is able to make all favor abound towards you. No matter what situation you may be in and no matter what you may encounter, God can began to release miracles on your behalf. The wind of miraculous favor takes us into the supernatural. Many of us our living lives on a natural life when a supernatural life is our portion.

The supernatural is our portion and miraculous favor takes us in to the supernatural. Miraculous favor brings forth divine intervention and unusual things happen. God revealed to me several instances when He released His miraculous favor.

Aaron - Miraculous Favor, Swallows Up Your Enemies

The favor of God will empower you to be a miracle, sign and a wonder and it will force your enemies to obey the commandments of God. Moses and Aaron had the favor of God on their lives and this was shown by their special assignment to ensure that God's people were liberated from a life of captivity. The favor of God also gives you power over ungodly spiritual activity and victory over your enemies. In fact, when God is on your side your challengers are swallowed up!

And Moses and Aaron went in unto Pharaoh, and they did so as the Lord had commanded: and Aaron cast down his rod before Pharaoh, and before his servants, and it became a serpent. Then Pharaoh also called the wise men and the sorcerers: now the magicians of Egypt, they also did in like manner with their enchantments. For they cast down every man his rod, and they became serpents: but Aaron's rod swallowed up their rods. - Exodus 7:10-12

The wind of miraculous favor is going to blow over your life and by the finger of God you will cast out devils and defeat your enemies (Luke 11:20). When times became tough Moses thought he had lost the favor of God (Numbers 11:11), but difficulties do not cancel your favor they simply push you to cry out to God for help. I believe the Lord answered Moses' cry by giving him help, the seventy elders (Numbers 11:16). God also performed a miracle, but the miracle was based on the posture of the people - complaining instead of praying. Israel left Egypt seeing miracles and favor and as soon as times became tough they complained. Let the God of Favor, the God of Miracles, bless you, shine the light of his favor on you and keep the faith through the process.

Mary – Miraculous Favor, Raises Your Level of Favor

Mary was shocked when she was told that she would give birth to the Son of God. God is going to shock you just like He shocked Mary! You are going to be shocked by the miracles that God does in your life.

These miracles are going to be astronomical to others, but it is also going to be mind blowing to you. God is ready to release mind blowing favor. The wind of miraculous favor that God is releasing will amaze you and astonish others. The favor is going to be so great that it will feel "out-of-this-world"! Because God is releasing a wind of miraculous favor upon the lives of people just like you, you will be in awe of God and start asking the following questions just like Mary asked:

You: How could this be, God?

You: How can this happen to me?

You: How can you do this unto me?

God: You have found favor in My sight.

God wants to amaze you with His favor. Favor is coming upon the people of God and many individuals will declare "I can't believe what the Lord has done". People will declare "God, that is incredible". The miraculous wind of favor is marvelous; it is astounding. The wind of miraculous favor is phenomenal; it bring forth angelic activity and unimagined unique opportunities for you to obey God for things that may seem insane. The wind of miraculous favor requires faith for the fulfillment of prophecies that the average person would consider foolish. This level favor is incredible. This level of favor gives you the ability to do things that no one else has the ability to do. As I wrote this book I heard "I am moving people into this miraculous level of favor so that people may know that I Am."

Paul – Miraculous Favor, Working of Unusual Miracles

An emerging generation of Christians are about to have authentic encounters with the Lord and experience a miraculous move of God. The wind of miraculous favor is about to blow over the misfits, misused and misunderstood. "Not only will people experience miracles, but they will also see miraculous, signs and wonders in ministry," says the Lord.

Paul was a misfit, but he was faithful to the assignment God gave him and as a result the wind of miraculous favor blew over his life. Paul was a misfit among the apostles. Paul did not walk with Jesus among the other apostles. If there was a poll among Christians at that time, Paul would have been voted "least likely to preach the gospel" because he zealously persecuted Believers. However, Paul had one encountered with the Lord on Damascus Road and his life was changed (Acts 9). Paul tried to preach to the Jews like the other apostles, but God was doing something different and Paul's assignment was an integral part of God's plan to reach the Gentiles (Acts 13:42). Despite the challenges he experienced, Paul knew who was in God.

> Paul, an apostle, (not of men, neither by man, but by Jesus Christ, and God the Father, who raised him from the dead;) - Galatians 1:1(KJV)

Paul was unstoppable! Paul's ministry is known for unusual miracles. Paul's process to ministry was not like the other apostles, but it prepared him to do what God called him to do and that was to reached the unreached.

Paul's ministry was surrounded by the wind of miraculous favor and it blew so strongly over his life that the following miracles manifested.

> And now, behold, the hand of the Lord is upon thee, and thou shalt be blind, not seeing the sun for a season. And immediately there fell on him a mist and a darkness; and he went about seeking some to lead him by the hand. Acts 13:11

> God was performing extraordinary miracles by the hands of Paul, so that handkerchiefs or aprons were even carried from his body to the sick, and the diseases left them and the evil spirits went out. - Acts 19:11-12 (NKJV)

> And Paul went down, and fell on him, and embracing him said, Trouble not yourselves; for his life is in him. When he therefore was come up again, and had broken bread, and eaten, and talked a long while, even till break of day, so he departed. And they brought the young man alive, and were not a little comforted. - Acts 20:10-12

> And when Paul had gathered a bundle of sticks, and laid them on the fire, there came a viper out of the heat, and fastened on his hand. And when the barbarians saw the venomous beast hang on his hand, they said among themselves, No doubt this man is a murderer, whom, though he hath escaped the sea, yet vengeance suffereth not to live. And he shook off the beast into the fire, and felt no harm. - Acts 28:3-5

And it came to pass, that the father of Publius lay sick of a fever and of a bloody flux: to whom Paul entered in, and prayed, and laid his hands on him, and healed him. - Acts 28:8

The wind of miraculous favor is an activation wind, it activates miracles, signs and wonders. Favor with God gives you the ability to walk in a level of authority that is so great that women and men stand in awe of God when they look at your life. You must remember that winds in the bible are symbolic of the manifest presence of God, the breathe of God and when God is in the midst of a situation miracles happen.

Lazarus - Miraculous Favor, Destroys Death

The wind of miraculous favor blew in Lazarus life and he was raised from the dead. Lazarus life was surrounded by the winds of favor and this is evident by his relationship with Jesus Christ the Messiah. Lazarus and Jesus were friends. Because Jesus walked in favor, He was able to extend favor to Lazarus. Within Jesus was the power and authority to defeat death and He demonstrated this power by only saying "Lazarus, come forth" and Lazarus was raised from the dead.

And when he thus had spoken, he cried with a loud voice, Lazarus, come forth. And he that was dead came forth, bound hand and foot with grave clothes: and his face was bound about with a napkin. Jesus saith unto them, Loose him, and let him go. - John 11: 43, 44 (KJV)

The spoken word of Jesus Christ, the very breath of God within Him, was released into the atmosphere and the winds of favor called Lazarus forth from the dead.

We see another example of miracles, wind, speaking, prophecy and victory over death in the Book of Ezekiel. God commanded Ezekiel to prophesy to the breath and this impacts an army of dry bones (Ezekiel 37:4). After Ezekiel prophesied the dry bones came alive;God told him to prophesy to the wind and command the four winds to breathe upon them that were slain (Ezekiel 37:9). Ezekiel prophesied and the winds blew and miraculously a great army arose.

> Then said he unto me, Prophesy unto the wind, prophesy, son of man, and say to the wind, Thus saith the Lord God; Come from the four winds, O breath, and breathe upon these slain, that they may live. So I prophesied as he commanded me, and the breath came into them, and they lived, and stood up upon their feet, an exceeding great army. - Ezekiel 37:9,10 (KJV)

The four winds breathed upon the skeletons and a great army rose up. The winds of God are blowing even now and the dry, discouraged and disengaged people spiritually dying are about to arise as the radical army of God. The winds of favor are blowing. "The wind of miraculous favor is blowing and dead dreams will be resurrected. The wind of miraculous favor is blowing and lives will change" says the Lord.

Hezekiah – Miraculous Favors, The Humble Prospers

The wind of miraculous favor not only causes miracle healing and restoration, it causes miracle money to come your way. People who humble themselves in the sight of the Lord position themselves for "exceeding much riches and honor" (2 Chronicles 32:26). As mentioned throughout this book, the winds in the bible reflect the very presence of God. There is no lack in the presence of God so as we humble ourselves before His throne of grace and the Spirit of God flows in our lives, a life of lack can miraculously become a life of luxury. Humility is the key to the winds of favor blowing in your life, especially miraculous favor.

> Notwithstanding Hezekiah humbled himself for the pride of his heart, both he and the inhabitants of Jerusalem, so that the wrath of the Lord came not upon them in the days of Hezekiah. And Hezekiah had exceeding much riches and honour: and he made himself treasuries for silver, and for gold, and for precious stones, and for spices, and for shields, and for all manner of pleasant jewels; Storehouses also for the increase of corn, and wine, and oil; and stalls for all manner of beasts, and cotes for flocks. Moreover he provided him cities, and possessions of flocks and herds in abundance: for God had given him substance very much. This same Hezekiah also stopped the upper watercourse of Gihon, and brought it straight down to the west side of

the city of David. And Hezekiah prospered in all his works. - 2 Chronicles 32:26-30 (KJV)

Pride will hinder the winds of favor from blowing over your life. God resists the proud, but He gives grace (favor) to the humble (James 4:6; 2 Peter 5:5). If you want the winds of favor to blow over your life, you must examine yourself. If God reveals that there's any pride in you humble yourself like Hezekiah did (2 Chronicles 32:26). Hezekiah humbled himself because of the pride in his heart and as a result not only was the wrath of God turned away, but the wind of miraculous favor blew and positioned him for great wealth. After Hezekiah humbled himself we see that "God had given him substance very much." The winds of favor will change your financial situation because God himself will give you substance. God will open the windows of heaven and money will miraculously comes into your life.

The wind of miraculous favor turns your life around. You can expect the impossible to happen in your life when you humble yourself before God's throne of grace and wait on him to lift you up. When the wind of miraculous favor blows in your life you understand that you have found favor in God's sight.

Prophetic Encouragement and Prophecy:

This miraculous favor is going to do what no man can do. God said I am releasing this miraculous favor and it is going to turn your life around.

God is releasing a miraculous favor so that whatever you put your hand on will prosper for His glory. Your ministry is going to prosper. Your life is going to prosper. Your bank account is going to prosper. Your seed and your seed's are going to prosper because of the miraculous favor of God. This type of favor, miraculous favor, only comes upon those who will remain humble in the sight of the Lord.

It is time to do a self-check. God, am I walking in favor? God, am I giving you the glory and honor that is due Your name? God am I blessing you? Am I returning favor through my prayers, petitions, and releasing favor unto others.

God grants us favor so that we can be vessels for Him to release favor. When we release favor unto others it brings glory and honor unto God. Why? Because He is the conduit of favor, He can trust us with His favor.

God is releasing this miraculous favor and He is going to do it in an astounding way. God said, I am about to shock you. I am about to do some things in your life that are just going to be in awe of Me. You are going to be in awe of who I AM. I am about to reveal to you that I AM that I AM in your life, in your situation - your impossible situations. I am about to show you what I am made of and I am about to show you what happens when My hand is upon your life.

- FAVOR MEDITATION -

*Therefore He who supplies the Spirit to you and works
miracles among you, does He do it by the works of the
law, or by the hearing of faith?— 6 just as Abraham
"believed God, and it was accounted to him for
righteousness." 7 Therefore know that only those who
are of faith are sons of Abraham. 8 And the Scripture,
foreseeing that God would justify the Gentiles by
faith, preached the gospel to Abraham beforehand,
saying, "In you all the nations shall be blessed." 9 So
then those who are of faith are blessed with believing
Abraham. - Galatians 3:5-9 (KNJV)*

12

WINDS OF FAVOR

Then said he unto me, Prophesy unto the wind, prophesy, son of man, and say to the wind, Thus saith the Lord God; Come from the four winds, O breath, and breathe upon these slain, that they may live. - Ezekiel 37:9

Prophesy to the winds. Open you mouth and proclaim that winds of favor our blowing strongly over your life. Winds are unseen, but powerful and strong so they are a great depiction of an unseen God. Biblically, wind is the unseen power and presence of God on the earth. In Hebrew, the word "wind" and breath" are both the same word, "Ruach" (Strong's #7307) and it is defined as "to breathe, blow, primarily denotes the wind; breath". In Ezekiel 37, Prophet Ezekiel was commanded to prophesy to the wind and he prophesied for the four winds to come. Ezekiel prophesied to the wind and the breath of God came into the a valley of dry bones and an exceedingly great army arose (Ezekiel 37:7-10). As you prophesy to the wind the winds of favor will blow and dead dreams will come alive again, dead visions will come alive again; God will breathe life in things that can be resurrected. God will reveal Himself and His power in the wind.

Winds of favor are an image of God's presence on the earth. God's presence may be revealed in one particular kind of wind or a combination of winds. For example, on the day of Pentecost, suddenly there was a sound like a mighty rushing wind (Acts 2:2). As I wrote this book, I literally heard the sound of a mighty rushing wind sometimes. I heard the powerful sounds of the winds of favor.

Winds are present within the context of extraordinary events happening in the bible. The extraordinary events are foreseen by God's servants, the prophets, through visions or by revelation. Winds in the bible are associated with unusual, unprecedented and even devastating events. However, winds are usually mentioned in connection with prophets of God or prophetic activity. This book is entitled "Winds of Favor" because it is a book that provides prophetic insight on the presence and power of God in someone's life. As such, you need to pray for the fulfillment of the words written in this book just as you would pray for the fulfillment any other prophecy.

In the King James Version of the bible, the phrase "four winds" is mentioned 9 times, the word "winds" 22 times and the word "wind" 178 times. The direction of the wind also has significance as noted below.

East wind:

This wind destroys, comes with crisis, brings judgment

> And the seven thin and ill favoured kine that came up after them are seven years; and the seven empty ears blasted with the east wind shall be seven years of famine.
> - Genesis 41:27 (see also: Exodus 12:13)

West wind:

This wind brings deliverance, refreshing and restoration

> And the Lord turned a mighty strong west wind, which took away the locusts, and cast them into the Red sea; there remained not one locust in all the coasts of Egypt. - Exodus 10:19

North wind:

This brings rain, blessing

> The north wind brings forth rain, And a backbiting tongue an angry countenance. - Proverbs 25:23 (NKJV)

South wind:

This wind brings peace, prosperity

> "Awake, O north wind, And come, south wind [blow softly upon my garden]; Make my garden breathe out fragrance, [for the one in whom my soul delights], Let its spices flow forth. Let my beloved come into his garden and eat its choicest fruits." - Songs 4:16

Winds are significant and when the winds of God began to blow powerful things happen. An angel told Zechariah that there were four winds that presented themselves before the Lord.

> And the angel answered me, These are the four winds or spirits of the heavens, which go forth from presenting themselves before the Lord of all the earth. - Zechariah 6:5 (AMP)

God determines the direction of winds and they do not blow except God commands the winds to blow. Accordingly, when the winds of favor began to blow over your life you can expect God to do something great because not only do God directs the winds, He creates the wind (Amos 4:3). Winds are God's messengers (Psalms 104:4).

> Who makes winds His messengers, flames of fire His ministers. Psalms 104:4(AMP)

Because the bible says that winds are messengers of God, we know that God speaks through the wind. God brings forth the wind from His storehouse (Jeremiah 10:13). You can go before God's throne of favor and ask Him to bring forth the winds of favor from His storehouse.

Winds obey the Lord. If winds need to be activated in your life God, as a prophet or prophetic minister, you can t speak to the wind (Ezekiel 37:9). If the winds need to be quieted because they are causing trouble, the Lord can rebuke the wind (Mathew 8:26).

> But He said to them, "Why are you fearful,
> O you of little faith?" Then He arose and
> rebuked the winds and the sea, and there was
> a great calm. So the men marveled, saying,
> "Who can this be, that even the winds and
> the sea obey Him?"
> -Mathew 8:26-27 (NKJV)

The winds of God are about to blow strongly. A wind from the Lord can spring up (Numbers 11:31). If you need a wind of favor to spring up in your life ask for it! God brings for the the wind out of His treasures.

> Whatsoever the Lord pleased, that did he in
> heaven, and in earth, in the seas, and all deep
> places. He causeth the vapours to ascend
> from the ends of the earth; he maketh
> lightnings for the rain; he bringeth the wind
> out of his treasuries. - Psalms 135: 6.7

God brings the wind out of His treasures. There is a double portion grace that comes upon the people of God when the winds of favor begin to flow. God will bring forth the winds out of His treasures because He is a great God. God will also release the treasures of darkness.

> And I will give thee the treasures of
> darkness, and hidden riches of secret places,
> that thou mayest know that I, the Lord,
> which call thee by thy name, am the God of
> Israel. - Isaiah 45:3 (KJV)

God wants the winds of favor to blow into your life from every direction. God knows the specific winds that need to blow in your life in order for you to arise.

Because God wants to bless you, because He takes pleasure in the prosperity of His servants (Psalms 35:27) and because He will give His sons and daughters the desires of their heart if we delight in him (Psalms 37:4) we can expect the blessings of God to come upon our lives when the winds of favor

Prophetic Exhortation & Prophecy:

There is strong wind of favor that is about to blow over those who believe the Lord our God and the prophets of God. Those that believe in the Lord will be established; those who believe in His prophets will prosper. Surely, there is a mighty rushing wind of favor blowing.

The winds of God are about to blow over your life. Prophesy to the four winds as I told Ezekiel and I will breathe new life into to your dreams and visions says the Lord. Your enemies have tried to kill your dreams and visions, but I am dealing with dream killers and I am resuscitating and reawakening your dream and visions with My fresh wind. My wind of deliverance is blowing to deliver you from the opinions of man and release you out your bondage. I'm about to breathe on you, I'm about to blow on you life and you will feel my favor. I command My winds of favor to blow on you! My winds of favor are blowing says God and the things you could not do in the past, My favor will do for you in the days ahead.

My winds of favor are here to refresh you. This wind of favor is a wind of change. This wind of favor is a wind that will transform your life.

This wind is about to orchestrate new opportunities for you and new open doors for you. Yes, this wind of favor will open new doors for you and no man can shut these doors. New moments of favor are coming upon you because winds of favor are surrounding you.

- FAVOR MEDITATION -

Whatsoever the Lord pleased, that did he in heaven, and in earth, in the seas, and all deep places. He causeth the vapours to ascend from the ends of the earth; he maketh lightnings for the rain; he bringeth the wind out of his treasuries. - Psalms 135: 6.7

ABOUT THE AUTHOR

Michelle J. Miller is an ambassador of Jesus Christ, global corporate attorney and global speaker who

 understands the power and responsibility of being a voice to and for others. Michelle walks in a strong apostolic prayer, prophetic and teaching anointing and she has a grace to ignite people in their gifts and call. Michelle's desire is to impact the world with her words. Michelle obtained her undergraduate degree from the University of Illinois at Urbana Champaign, her law degree from DePaul University College of Law and her advanced law degree (LLM) from the John Marshall Law School. Michelle has a Certification in Chinese Law and she is an Illinois licensed Managing Real Estate Broker. Michelle is a Certified Ministering Spiritual Gifts Instructor and she also holds a Doctorate of Ministry in Theology. Michelle loves to encourage others to pursue their visions and dreams with passion and persistence. Michelle is a global visionary and whether you are a young adult seeking to develop your life vision or an experienced leaders looking to hone you skills, you will find that you'll be able to excel with Michelle. Michelle has been to several nations and she believes that God will continue to use her as an example of God's chosen ones being able to go from the neighborhood to the

nations. Michelle is under the spiritual leadership of Apostle John Eckhardt, Overseer and Senior Pastor of Crusaders Church in Chicago, Illinois. Michelle J. Miller resides in the Chicago area with her daughter, Heaven S. Miller.

43326603R00070

Made in the USA
Lexington, KY
27 June 2019